CLASS 37 LOCOMOTIVES

Andrew Walker

John Walker | Vaughan Hellam

Acknowledgements

The author and publisher would like to thank John Walker and Vaughan Hellam for permission to use copyrighted material in this book. All other photographs are by the author.

First published 2016

Amberley Publishing
The Hill, Stroud
Gloucestershire, GL5 4EP

www.amberley-books.com

Copyright © Andrew Walker, 2016

The right of Andrew Walker to be identified as the Author of this work has been asserted in accordance with the Copyrights, Designs and Patents Act 1988.

ISBN 978 1 4456 5737 0 (print)
ISBN 978 1 4456 5738 7 (ebook)

All rights reserved. No part of this book may be reprinted or reproduced or utilised in any form or by any electronic, mechanical or other means, now known or hereafter invented, including photocopying and recording, or in any information storage or retrieval system, without the permission in writing from the Publishers.

British Library Cataloguing in Publication Data.
A catalogue record for this book is available from the British Library.

Typesetting by Amberley Publishing.
Printed in the UK.

Foreword

Well-proportioned, versatile, aesthetic, durable. The English Electric Class 37, the great survivor of the British Modernisation Plan diesel fleet, deserves all of these accolades and more. They have never been as celebrated as the Deltics, nor as idolised as the Westerns, and every one of them was nameless at the outset – yet, this is the locomotive that has in many ways surpassed its more illustrious peers as an example of all that is best in motive power design and engineering. I was born in 1962, while these pleasant-looking machines were still rolling out of the construction shops, and I grew up to their sound. Living alongside the Barnsley–Penistone line, the beat of their exhaust, day and night, was part of the soundtrack of childhood. The greatest drama of all was provided by D6710, summoned from Wath depot on a June night in 1969 to rescue *Flying Scotsman*, marooned on the gradient out of Barnsley station with its passenger special bound for Huddersfield. What are the odds on 'the most famous engine' coming to a stand opposite a boy's bedroom window? It was like a story from the Rev. W. Awdry. *Troublesome Engines* indeed. So it was difficult to ignore the Class 37s and, when I took up railway photography in 1978, there always seemed to be plenty of them about. Over the following thirty (and more) years I took many pictures, but never enough. Many of what I did take are presented in this pictorial collection, together with some excellent examples from two other enthusiasts, John M. Walker and Vaughan Hellam, to whom I give my grateful thanks.

Introduction

It was only when the 'second generation' of Modernisation Plan diesel types was ordered by the British Transport Commission that Type 3 locomotives featured in the fleet. Following in the wake of the BRCW Class 33 and the Beyer-Peacock 'Hymek', the Class 37s built by both English Electric at its Vulcan Foundry and by Robert Stephenson & Hawthorns eventually amounted to 309 examples by the time construction finished in 1965. Visually similar to its Type 4 cousin the Class 40, the 37s were initially allocated to Eastern, North Eastern and Western regions and quickly earned a reputation for dependability that saw the fleet achieve excellent availability in traffic on both freight and passenger operations. Like the 40s, the first locomotives were built with central nose-end gangway doors, which were subsequently deemed unnecessary. The later central headcode panel gave a nicely balanced and clean frontal appearance.

Over 300 Class 37s were in traffic by the mid-1960s, and the fleet soon began to demonstrate its capability with intensive rostering on freight and passenger services across England and Wales. A pair of Class 37s was a particularly potent traction resource, and the increasing prevalence of high-capacity block freight in the 1970s, notably in the coal and steel industries, but also in oil and aggregates, meant that this combination became a fixture in many parts of the country. Elsewhere, single Class 37s were highly effective on Eastern Region passenger turns out of London Liverpool Street and became the dominant force on the Cambridge and Kings Lynn routes. By the mid-1980s, the fleet was allocated to all regions except the Southern, but 37s regularly appeared there. It was truly a ubiquitous locomotive.

After twenty years or so of intensive use, the Class 37 fleet was selected for a major refurbishment programme at BREL Crewe, from which they emerged with new electrical and auxiliary equipment, rebuilt engines and a number of other important modifications that facilitated more flexible operation and which extended their working life well into the late 1990s and beyond. When the new generation of North American diesel imports began to appear on British metals it came as no surprise that the numbers of Class 37s began to diminish, with a growing cohort finding its way into the hands of dedicated preservationists, sometimes after returning from service across the English Channel. Such was their resilience, however, that even as I write this in 2016, several are still at work on the national network, sporting more modifications and yet retaining all the essential elements of that original, well balanced, well tempered design.

Andrew Walker
Nottingham

D6700 (Nos 37119/37350) at Toton Depot

The progenitor of the fleet, D6700, was built at Vulcan Foundry in December 1960 and was delivered new to Stratford. It was later named *NRM National Railway Museum* and in 2004 it went into preservation on the North Yorkshire Moors Railway. Here it is at Toton in August 1998.

No. 37350 at Whitley Bridge

This is D6700, after its second renumbering from 37119, heading oil tanks at Whitley Bridge on 15 April 1993. Here No. 37350 features a shortened front valance and plated-over nose, modifications that were later reversed. (J. M. Walker)

No. 37226 at Royston Junction

No. 37226 of Tinsley depot meanders across misty Royston Junction on the former Midland main line with a scrap metal working in December 1982. This was around seven years before it was renumbered to 37379, and twenty-six years before it, too, was consigned to the scrapyard.

No. 37254 at Twyford

No. 37254 heads a lengthy train of open-sided wagons at Twyford on a grim 23 January 1988. This Vulcan Foundry machine was delivered new as D6954 in 1965 and was sold for preservation in 1999. Named *Driver Robin Prince M.B.E* at Tunbridge Wells West in 2009, it was still in traffic in 2016.

No. 37034 at Guide Bridge

No. 37034 takes a block load of hoppers through Guide Bridge on 26 May 1982. This locomotive was built at Vulcan Foundry and was released to traffic as D6734 in March 1962. It was later rebuilt and numbered 37704, at which point the characteristic headcode boxes were removed and sealed-beam marker lights fitted.

No. 37401 at Oban

This is Oban in July 1990, and No. 37401 *Mary Queen of Scots* stands at the head of a rake of oil tanks in the terminus. Built at Vulcan Foundry in February 1965 as D6968, it was first allocated to Darnall. Under the TOPS programme it became No. 37268, and then No. 37401 in 1985. It was withdrawn in 2013 and preserved at the Bo'ness Railway, but was brought back onto the national network as part of the DRS fleet in 2015.

No. 37215 at Toddington

No. 37215 rests between duties at Toddington on the Gloucestershire & Warwickshire Railway in May 1999. This Vulcan Foundry machine was delivered new as D6915 in January 1964 and was withdrawn in 1993. Bought by the Growler Group in 1994, it is still in traffic.

No. 37255 at Quorn

No. 37255, in faded 'Dutch' Civil Engineer's livery, languishes in open storage on the Great Central Railway at Quorn in 2010. This is a Vulcan Foundry built machine, emerging from the works in January 1965 as D6955.

No. 37073 at Doncaster Works

No. 37073 stands in the paint shop yard at Doncaster Works in 1985. Built at Robert Stephenson & Hawthorns (RSH) in September 1962 as D6773, its first home depot was Thornaby. It spent time in France from 1999 to 2000 but, on its return, survived only another three years before being scrapped at Bury.

No. 37219 at Basford Hall Yard, Crewe

No. 37219 stands next to No. 58050 at Basford Hall on 27 August 1995. No. 37219 was built at Vulcan Foundry and entered traffic in January 1964 as D6919. Withdrawn in 2005, it moved to the Gloucestershire Warwickshire Railway and was later named *Shirley Ann Smith*.

No. 37055 at Stratford

Full-length valance, nose-end doors and 'domino' headcode panels give No. 37055 a classic late-1970s look as it speeds through Stratford in October 1979 with a London-bound passenger service. This was one of the Vulcan Foundry build, released to traffic in September 1962 as D6755 and withdrawn from service in 2008.

No. 37887 at Doncaster Works

During its first overhaul since conversion to one of the 120-ton 'heavyweight' variants, No. 37887 is seen at Doncaster Works on 12 July 1992. This loco was originally D6820, built at the RSH foundry in March 1963. It became No. 37120 in 1974 and then No. 37887 in 1988.

No. 37226 at Summer Lane, Barnsley

In the Woodhead era it was unusual to see MGR workings on the Barnsley–Dodworth route, as trains normally travelled via the electrified Worsborough line. Consequently, this shot of No. 37226 in July 1979 is something of a rarity. It was renumbered to 37379 in 1989 and acquired the name *Ipswich WRD Quality Approved* in 1994.

No. 37124 at Burton upon Trent

Tinsley's No. 37124 heads through Burton with mineral wagons on 2 July 1979. This machine was built by RSH and was delivered new to Cardiff Canton in April 1963. In later life it became No. 37894, and was despatched to France for two years from 1999.

No. 37221 at Lincoln Central

In the work-stained condition typical of many of the fleet, No. 37221 is seen stabled in one of Lincoln's bay platforms in 1986. Built at Vulcan Foundry in January 1964 and first allocated to Landore depot, No. 37221 was hired out to France from 1999 to 2000 and was withdrawn and cut up at Booth's of Rotherham in 2009.

No. 37688 at Buxton

A line of Class 37s is seen here stabled outside Buxton station in August 1992. At the front is the aptly named No. 37688 *Great Rocks*. Built at Vulcan Foundry as D6905 (later No. 37205), it first turned a wheel in November 1963 and was allocated initially to Landore shed. It became No. 37688 in 1987.

No. 37505 at York

No. 37505 *British Steel Workington* passes York with a short freight in 1989. A Vulcan Foundry machine, it was delivered new to Stratford as D6728 in 1961. Later No. 37028, it assumed its new identity as No. 37505 in 1986, emerging from its rebuild at Crewe in Railfreight grey livery.

No. 37706 at Sowerby Bridge

No. 37706 passes Sowerby Bridge with Leeds–Stanlow empty oil tanks on 2 June 1993. One of the first few of the class to be built, it was released to traffic from Vulcan Foundry as D6716 in the summer of 1961. Under the TOPS scheme it became No. 37016 and was renumbered again to 37706 in 1987. (V. Hellam)

No. 37428 at Inverness

A Welshman in the Highlands – No. 37428 *David Lloyd George*, previously No. 37281, stands at the buffers at Inverness station on 24 August 1993. (J. M. Walker)

No. 37088 at Perth

On passenger duty despite the Civil Engineer's livery, No. 37088 *Clydesdale* is seen here at Perth on 10 July 1993. Built by RSH in 1963 as D6788, and delivered new to Gateshead, it became No. 37088 in 1974 and then No. 37323 in 1986, reverting back to No. 37088 in 1989. (V. Hellam)

No. 37006 at Oakenshaw, Wakefield

No. 37006 approaches Wakefield from the Knottingley direction at Oakenshaw in May 1982. This locomotive lost its twin headcode boxes when it was converted to No. 37798 in 1986. It remained in service until 2009 and was then scrapped at Booth's of Rotherham.

No. 37260 at Achnasheen

No. 37260 is seen here at Achnasheen on a Kyle of Lochalsh to Inverness service on 25 June 1985. Built at Vulcan Foundry in 1965, it went first to Darnall and then Wath in quick succession. Named *Radio Highland* in 1984, it was withdrawn only five years later, as a result of fire damage, and was cut up in 1991.

No. 37417 at Toton

No. 37417 *RAIL Magazine* was beautifully turned out for the Toton open weekend in August 1998. It was released to traffic from Vulcan Foundry as D6969 in 1965 and delivered new to Cardiff Canton. It became No. 37269 under the TOPS scheme and then No. 37417 in 1985, after which it carried the name *Highland Region*.

No. 37418 at Crewe Electric Depot

No. 37418 *East Lancashire Railway* looks immaculate in EWS livery at Crewe Electric Depot on 3 May 1997. This locomotive began life as D6971 in March 1965, and became No. 37418 in 1985. It was bought for preservation in 2007, appropriately becoming a resident at the ELR.

Nos 37602 and 37259 at Thornhill

Nos 37602 and 37259 pass Thornhill with empty ballast hoppers on 13 July 2014. No. 37259 carried the number 37388 for several years, but reverted to 37259 when it became part of the DRS fleet. No. 37602 started life as RSH-built D6782, then became No. 37082 and later No. 37502 before assuming its current identity. (V. Hellam)

No. 37059 at Attenborough

No. 37059 approaches Attenborough on 19 June 2015 on a light engine trip from Norwich to Loughborough's Brush foundry. Modular headlights and a smooth nose contrast with the appearance it would have presented when built as D6759 in October 1962. Later named *Port of Tilbury*, No. 37059 was sold by EWS in 2001, becoming part of the DRS fleet.

No. 37097 at Doncaster Works

A portrait of No. 37097 awaiting attention at Doncaster Works on 23 September 1984. In common with many of the twin-headcode machines, No. 37097 subsequently had the nose-end doors plated over. This locomotive survives in preservation on the Caledonian Railway. (J. M. Walker)

No. 37019 at Barnsley

Class 76s were occasionally taken to Wath via Barnsley if the electrified branch from Penistone was switched out, and that is probably what has happened here, as Tinsley's No. 37019 tows a quartet of EM1s through the station on 13 July 1981. No. 37019 began life as D6719 in 1961 and was scrapped in 2004 after several years of storage. (V. Hellam)

No. 37212 at Leyburn

37212 is seen here on the Redmire branch at Leyburn with a ballast working on 28 July 1983. In the second image the train is standing at Leyburn's disused station platform awaiting the signal to proceed towards Northallerton. Delivered new from Vulcan Foundry to Landore depot in 1964 as D6912, it was withdrawn from service in 2003 and cut up in 2004, forty years after its debut on the national network. (J. M. Walker)

No. 37211 at Tinsley

Looking smart in its Trainload Construction sub-sector livery, No. 37211 arrives on shed at Tinsley on 10 April 1993. (J. M. Walker)

No. 37420 at Tinsley depot

No. 37420 *The Scottish Hosteller* stands in the shed yard at Tinsley on 8 June 1993. One of the last to be built, No. 37420 was released to traffic from Vulcan Foundry as D6997 in the summer of 1965. It was renumbered to 37297 in 1974, and then became No. 37420 after a heavy general overhaul in 1985.

No. 37511 at Rotherham

No. 37511 has just passed Rotherham Road sidings and is heading south towards Tinsley with empty steel bolsters on 7 April 1993. Previously No. 37103, this locomotive later became No. 37607. (J. M. Walker)

Nos 37040 and 37048 at Barnsley

The Co-op's imposing warehouse at Summer Lane forms the backdrop to this shot of Nos 37040 and 37048 on a Dodworth–Wath MGR working in April 1985. Both machines emerged from Vulcan Foundry in the summer of 1962. No. 37048 was cut up at Toton in 2003, with No. 37040 lasting another three years.

Nos 37899 and 37896 at Brookhouse, South Yorkshire

No. 37899 *Sir Gorllewin Morgannwg/County of West Glamorgan* and No. 37896 head the Bolsover Balladeer at Brookhouse in South Yorkshire, on 1 September 1991. No. 37896 was built at Vulcan Foundry in 1964 as D6891. It became No. 37231 under the TOPS scheme and then No. 37896 in 1986. No. 37899, built in 1964 as D6931, became No. 37161 under the TOPS system and was later hired to Spain. Destined never to return to the UK, it was cut up in Madrid in 2003.

Nos 37307 and 37080 at Guide Bridge

Nos 37080 and 37307 make their way onto Guide Bridge holding sidings on 16 April 1983. No. 37307 later became No. 37403 and has carried no fewer than three names: *Isle of Mull*, *Glendarroch* and *Ben Cruachan*. It was sold for preservation in 2008. Its partner No. 37080, an RSH machine of 1962 vintage, enjoyed no such illustrious career, being cut up at Cardiff in 1997. (J. M. Walker)

Nos 37197 and 37113 at Guide Bridge

Nos 37197 and 37113 double-head returning aggregate hoppers through Guide Bridge on 27 September 1983. No. 37197 later became No. 37375, while No. 37113, later named *Radio Highland* (a name previously carried No. by 37260), was an early withdrawal following a collision in 1994. (V. Hellam)

No. 37042 at Goose Hill Junction

A gloriously mixed freight trails across Goose Hill Junction at Normanton behind No. 37042 on 29 June 1983. A Vulcan Foundry machine built as D6742 in the summer of 1962, its first home base was Darnall. No. 37042 was sold to preservation in 2011 and subsequently moved to the Eden Valley Railway. (V. Hellam)

No. 37187 at Princes Risborough

No. 37187 stands with a train of tube stock at Princes Risborough on 20 April 1984. Built by RSH as D6887 in 1964, it later became No. 37683 and served in France from 1999 to 2000. It survived for a further thirteen years and was cut up Booth's of Rotherham in 2013. (V. Hellam)

No. 37293 at Cardiff

No. 37293 is seen at Cardiff station on 17 December 1983, in charge of the Canton steam crane. Built at Vulcan Foundry as D6993 in 1965, it served in France from 1999 to 2000, but on its return was destined to spend only a further nine years in traffic. (J. M. Walker)

No. 37107 at Newcastle Central

No. 37107 takes the avoiding lines at Newcastle with a train of ammonia tanks on 9 February 1985. Seen here in the all-pervading rail blue, No. 37107 later carried Civil Engineer's livery and was unofficially named *Fury*. It was scrapped in 2001. (J. M. Walker)

No. 37716 at Nottingham

No. 37716 *British Steel Corby* is caught in a shaft of sunlight at Nottingham station while going east with empty oil tanks in 1993. Built at Vulcan Foundry, No. 37716 began life as D6794. It was renumbered to 37094 late in 1973 and then 37716 in 1988.

No. 37174 at Ickles Yard, Rotherham

Seen here in the steel-making heartland of the Don Valley, No. 37174 rests between shunting duties at Ickles Yard at Rotherham. Released to traffic from Vulcan Foundry as D6874 in September 1963, No. 37174 endured until sold for scrap in 2007. (J. M. Walker)

No. 37667 at Toton

Thornaby-based No. 37667 is seen here stabled at Toton depot on 13 August 1988. Delivered new to Cardiff Canton depot from Vulcan Foundry as D6851 in July 1963, this locomotive became No. 37151 in 1974 and then No. 37667 in 1988. It was later named *Wensleydale*.

Nos 37030 and 37067 at Barnsley

Split-headcode pair Nos 37030 and 37067 turn on the power as they haul a loaded MGR service from Dodworth through Barnsley on 11 May 1983. Coal from Dodworth was routed this way following the closure of the Woodhead route in 1981. No. 37030 later became No. 37701, while No. 37067 became No. 37703. (V. Hellam)

No. 37027 at Edale

No. 37027 stands in the loop at Edale station on 9 March 1986, with crash-damaged No. 31436 in tow. No. 37027 was released to traffic in September 1961 as D6727, and in later life was renumbered to 37519, losing the twin headcode boxes and snowploughs following its refurbishment at Crewe. (V. Hellam)

Nos 37076 and 37249 at Cudworth

With the heat haze from their exhausts blurring the semaphores at Cudworth South Junction, Nos 37076 and 37249 head a northbound MGR working in August 1981. No. 37076 survives in service as No. 37518, but No. 37249, after being renumbered to 37903 following refurbishment at Crewe, was withdrawn and cut up in 2005. (V. Hellam)

Nos 37040 and 37048 at Ecclesfield

On 2 April 1985, Nos 37040 and 37048 power past Ecclesfield with a loaded MGR working from Dodworth. Both locomotives were released to traffic from Vulcan Foundry in the summer of 1962, and survived in service until 2000 and 1996 respectively.

Nos 37226 and 37218 at Dodworth

A summer's evening at Dodworth in 1982, with two of Tinsley's allocation, Nos 37226 and 37218, pulling away from the colliery with a loaded MGR service for Wath. No. 37226 was cut up at Booth's of Rotherham in 2008, but No. 37218 was still in traffic in 2015, more than fifty years after it emerged from Vulcan Foundry early in 1964.

Nos 37176 and 37189 at Swindon

A loaded aggregates train storms through Swindon station behind Nos 37176 and 37189 on 15 February 1983. No. 37176 later became No. 37883, and was hired out to Spain where it was scrapped in 2011; No. 37189 became No. 37672 and although it survived a cross-Channel tour of duty, this time in France, it was later cut up at Stockton. (J. M. Walker)

No. 37798 at Barnetby

No. 37798, the former No. 37006, and pictured here in Railfreight sector livery, heads through Barnetby with returning empty oil tanks for Immingham on 2 August 1993. Conversion to a 37/7 took place at Crewe in 1986. (J. M. Walker)

No. 37115 at Wakefield Kirkgate

No. 37115 heads through Wakefield Kirkgate in May 1982. Later modifications saw the headcode boxes removed and front doors plated, with recessed headlights. This was the second of four identities for D6815. It carried the number 37115 for thirteen years, becoming No. 37514 in 1987 then No. 37609 in 1995.

No. 37715 at Sowerby Bridge

A Stanlow–Leeds oil service heads through Sowerby Bridge on a misty August morning in 1993. No. 37715 was built at Vulcan Foundry as D6721 in July 1961 and later became No. 37021 under the TOPS scheme. Renumbering to 37715 came in 1988, and it was named twice in 1993, first as *British Steel Teeside* and then *British Petroleum*. (V. Hellam)

No. 37031 at Mirfield

No. 37031 heads a rake of mineral wagons through Mirfield on 30 November 1979. Built at Vulcan Foundry in October 1961, it emerged from the factory as D6731, and was first allocated to Hull. Renumbered to 37031 in 1974, it was a relatively early casualty, being cut up at Cardiff in 1997.

No. 37889 at Doncaster Works

An ex-works No. 37889 is seen here on display at the Doncaster Works open day of July 1992. Built as D6933 in 1964, and becoming No. 37233 under TOPS, this locomotive was converted to Class 37/7 specification at Crewe in 1987. After a period of storage from 1999, it was scrapped in 2007.

No. 37023 at Doveholes

No. 37023 works an empty ballast train at Doveholes in Derbyshire on 16 September 1984. This was an early Vulcan Foundry build, delivered new as D6723 in the summer of 1961. Named *Stratford TMD Quality Approved* in 1994, it later carried Civil Engineer's grey and Mainline's blue liveries. (J. M. Walker)

No. 37198 at Rotherham

Looking north from Rotherham Masborough on 27 August 1983, No. 37198 approaches on a summer Saturday service. The very last of the Robert Stephenson & Hawthorns batch, No. 37198 began life as D6898 in April 1964. It was sold for preservation in 2004. (J. M. Walker)

No. 37610 at Derby

DRS-liveried No. 37610 puts out a burst of exhaust as it approaches the station at Derby in the summer of 2002. This locomotive had three previous identities; built in 1963 as D6881, it became No. 37181 under the TOPS scheme and then No. 37687 in 1987. Its final renumbering came in 1995 when it became part of the EPS fleet.

Nos 37048 and 37057 at Barnsley

Nos 37048 and 37057 head an empty MGR service at Barnsley on 2 August 1983. Both were built at Vulcan Foundry, with No. 37048 emerging as D6748 and being delivered new to Darnall in September 1962. No. 37057 was delivered new to Thornaby as D6757 in October 1962, and after a lengthy career was sold by EWS to Harry Needle Railways, following which it was transferred to the Colas Railfreight fleet. (J. M. Walker)

No. 37089 at Oakenshaw Junction

Looking towards Wakefield from Oakenshaw in June 1982, No. 47349 waits for No. 37089 to cross its path with a mixed freight mainly comprising covered vans, bound for the Midland main line.

No. 37140 at Doncaster Works

Sporting familiar rail blue livery with black-and-white headcode panel, No. 37140 stands outside the 'Plant' at Doncaster on 26 February 1983. It later became part of the Civil Engineer's fleet and was wearing the trademark 'Dutch' grey-and-yellow livery at the time of its withdrawal in 1999. (J. M. Walker)

No. 37178 at Doncaster Works

Fresh out of the box – an immaculate No. 37178 stands outside the works following its refurbishment on 17 February 1983. The shortened front valance is readily apparent when compared with its pre-treatment sister No. 37140. After a period in storage, No. 37178 later became Network Rail's No. 97303, and is still in traffic in 2016. (J. M. Walker)

No. 37427 at Inverness

On 24 August 1993, No. 37427 *Highland Enterprise* is caught between the colour light signals at Inverness during a light engine move. It is in the relatively short-lived Regional Railways livery. Previously No. 37288, it had carried the name *Bont Y Bermo* from 1986 to 1993. (J. M. Walker)

No. 37798 at Derby

In Mainline blue livery, No. 37798 runs light engine through Derby in the summer of 2002. Its original headcode boxes have been removed and recessed headlights fitted. Built at Vulcan Foundry as D6706 in January 1961, it was delivered new to Norwich. It became No. 37006 in 1974 and then No. 37798 in 1986.

No. 37122 at Manchester Victoria

No. 37122 rests on a siding at Manchester Victoria station on 22 August 1983. Somewhat anonymous in corporate rail blue, No. 37122 later became two-tone grey-liveried No. 37692 and was named *The Lass o' Ballochmyle*. (J. M. Walker)

No. 37221 at Lincoln Central

No. 37221 finds a quiet parking spot at Lincoln Central station in this 1986 view. Built at Vulcan Foundry in January 1964, it was delivered new to Landore. Hired out to France from 1999 to 2000, it was withdrawn and cut up at Booth's of Rotherham in 2009.

No. 37024 at Rotherham Masborough

No. 37024 heads south through Rotherham Masborough in May 1982 with a train of flat wagons. As built, D6724 was a vacuum-brake only machine, but was converted to dual brakes in 1969.

No. 37103 at Rotherham

No. 37103 turns on the power as it heads off the Treeton line at Rotherham Masborough on 4 August 1984. This Vulcan Foundry machine later carried the number 37511 and then 37607, an identity it retained as part of the DRS fleet when allocated there in 2012. (J. M. Walker)

No. 37044 at Doncaster Works

No. 37044 attracts a crowd during the Doncaster Works Open Day in 1984. Built at Vulcan Foundry in June 1962, and first allocated to Darnall, it was selected for rebuilding as a heavyweight Class 37/7, emerging from Crewe as No. 37710 in 1988.

No. 37891 at Doncaster Works

Up on the jacks, the body of No. 37891 is seen here at Doncaster Works on 20 May 1990. Built by RSH as D6866 in June 1963 and delivered new to Cardiff Canton, it became No. 37166 in 1974 and then No. 37891 after refurbishment at Crewe in 1987. After service in France from 1999 to 2000 it lasted another decade before being cut up at Attercliffe. (V. Hellam)

No. 37095 at Attenborough

No. 37095 approaches Attenborough station from the Toton direction with a single cement wagon bound for the Blue Circle terminal at nearby Beeston on 21 July 1988. Withdrawn in 1999, No. 37095 was finally cut up in 2005.

No. 37100 at Doncaster Works

No. 37100 undergoes attention at Doncaster Works on 28 July 1984. The 101st of the fleet to be built, it emerged from Vulcan Foundry in December 1962 as D6800. It served in France from 1999 to 2000, subsequently becoming No. 97301 as part of Network Rail's departmental fleet. (J. M. Walker)

No. 37002 at Wakefield Kirkgate

No. 37002 brings an engineer's train into Wakefield Kirkgate on 5 December 1981. Only the third of the type to emerge from Vulcan Foundry, it was built in December 1960 and delivered new to Stratford. It underwent a change of identity to No. 37351 in 1989, and was withdrawn in 2007. (V. Hellam)

No. 37067 at Barnsley

No. 37067 stands at Barnsley Station Junction during an engineer's occupation on 22 May 1983. Built as D6767 in November 1962, it was later converted to a 37/7, emerging from the works in 1987 as No. 37703 in grey-and-yellow 'large logo' livery. (V. Hellam)

No. 37041 at Sheffield

Once an everyday South Yorkshire scene – No. 37041 waits on the centre roads at Sheffield with an acetic acid tank train, with Peak 45150 alongside, on 25 February 1985. Built as D6741 in the summer of 1962, No. 37041 was later renumbered to 37520. It was withdrawn and scrapped in 2007. (V. Hellam)

Nos 37216 and 37200 at New Mills South Junction

Nos 37216 and 37200 bring a train of hoppers off the Stockport line at New Mills South on 31 August 1984. These are both Vulcan Foundry machines. No. 37216 was built in January 1964 and was delivered new to Landore, later carrying the name *Great Eastern*. No. 37200 was built in October 1963 and delivered new to Cardiff Canton as D6900; it later became No. 37377. (J. M. Walker)

No. 37070 at Strafford Crossing

A truly historic image, showing the very last diesel-hauled freight to run over the Penistone–Wath line. This is No. 37070 at Strafford Crossing, heading towards Wath on 17 July 1981. An RSH machine built in August 1962, No. 37070 later carried Railfreight Distribution livery. It was withdrawn in 1996, but not cut up until 2004. (V. Hellam)

No. 37136 at Wath

As another member of the class departs on an eastbound empty hopper turn, Tinsley's No. 37136 approaches Wath Yard with a rake of mineral wagons in this 1982 image. This locomotive became Ruston engined No. 37905 just four years later. (V. Hellam)

No. 37187 at Sheffield

A superb summer afternoon at Sheffield sees No. 37187 waiting with empty stock on 25 August 1984. This RSH machine was built in 1964 and later became No. 37683. It was hired out to France in 1999 and served for a further decade on its return to the UK, being scrapped in 2013. (J. M. Walker)

Nos 37084 and 37380 at Great Rocks Junction

Light engines Nos 37084 and 37380 head away from Buxton in the direction of Peak Forest in this image from 17 June 1988. No. 37084 was renumbered to 37718 a year later following refurbishment at Crewe.

No. 37250 at Manchester Victoria

No. 37250 heads a short eastbound Speedlink service at Manchester Victoria on 20 August 1984. Built at Vulcan Foundry in 1964 and delivered new as D6950 to Cardiff Canton, it was one of numerous 37s that served in France at the turn of the century. Sold for preservation in 2008, it survives in service on the Wensleydale Railway. (J. M. Walker)

No. 37238 at Oakenshaw

No. 37238 heads a short freight away from Wakefield towards Crofton West Junction in June 1982. Built at Vulcan Foundry, this locomotive was delivered new to Cardiff Canton in June 1964. It carried the name *Spitfire Mk II* when based at Tinsley from 1990 to 1991, and was later hired out for duty in France.

No. 37283 at Sheffield

Sheffield station on 6 August 1983, with No. 37283 on a summer Saturday service for the East Coast. One of the RSH batch, it was delivered new to Cardiff Canton in March 1963. It was renumbered to 37895 after an overhaul at Crewe in 1987 and had a two-year stint on hire in Italy from 2001 to 2003. (J. M. Walker)

No. 37264 at Inverness

No. 37264 stands at Inverness with parcels stock on 25 June 1985. Like a number of the fleet delivered from Vulcan Foundry in early 1965, it went first to Darnall and was then transferred in short order to nearby Wath. It became a Scottish Region machine in 1982, and was sold for preservation in 2001.

No. 37069 at Colton Junction

No. 37069 heads south at Colton Junction with a bulk oil working. The very first RHS locomotive, No. 37069 emerged from the foundry as D6769 in July 1962. It was later named *Thornaby TMD*. It enjoyed a spell of duty in France from 1999 to 2000, and was then overhauled at Brush in Loughborough in 2003.

Nos 37077 and 37203 at Barnetby

Nos 37077 and 37203 pass Barnetby with iron ore empties on 22 April 1987. Split-box No. 37077 has a rather featureless frontal appearance, having had its nose-end doors removed. This locomotive was delivered new from RSH in 1962, and was one of the batch hired out to France between 1999 and 2000.

No. 37119 at Treeton South

No. 37119 heads towards Chesterfield at Treeton South on a steel slab working in April 1985. This locomotive is the class pioneer, formerly D6700. It became No. 37350 in March 1988 and was later preserved as part of the National Collection.

No. 37069 at Chesterfield

A bulk oil working goes south at Chesterfield behind No. 37069 on 24 August 1983. (J. M. Walker)

No. 37025 at Inverness

No. 37025 is seen here at Inverness prior to working a Kyle of Lochalsh service on 25 June 1982. Built at Vulcan Foundry and entering traffic in August 1961 as D6725, its first home depot was Stratford.

No. 37040 at Horbury

No. 37040 stands outside Healey Mills yard at Horbury with an engineer's working on 16 September 1984. (J. M. Walker)

Nos 37143 and 37168 at Manchester Victoria

Nos 37143 and 37168 power away from Manchester Victoria with bitumen tanks on 22 August 1983. No. 37143 was delivered new as D6843 in May 1963, renumbered to 37143 in 1974, then became No. 37800 in 1986 and carried the name *Glo Cymru* until 1994. No. 37168 was built as D6868 and delivered new from RSH in October 1963. It later became No. 37890 and was named *The Railway Observer*. (J. M. Walker)

No. 37067 at Barnsley

In April 1983, a Class 31/37 combination takes a loaded MGR working from Dodworth towards Barnsley, destined for Wath. No. 37067 was built at Vulcan Foundry in November 1962 as D6767. It was later rebuilt as a 37/7, carrying the number 37703. After a spell on hire to Spain from 2001 to 2004, No. 37703 returned to the UK and was later transferred to Carlisle Kingmoor as part of the DRS fleet.

Nos 37521, 37503, 37042 and 37689 at Doncaster shed

A quartet of withdrawn 37s stands at Doncaster shed in June 2009. No. 37521 was originally D6817; it became No. 37117 in 1974 and then No. 37521 in 1988. No. 37503 emerged from Vulcan Foundry as D6717, becoming No. 37017 in 1974 and then No. 37503 in 1986. It later carried the name *British Steel Shelton*. No. 37042 was built at Vulcan Foundry in June 1962, and was sold for preservation to the Eden Valley Railway. No. 37689 was not so fortunate. Built in March 1964 as D6895 (later No. 37195, then No. 37689 from 1987), it was cut up in 2011.

No. 37517 at Healey Mills

Healey Mills on 30 June 2006, and No. 37517 heads up a line of nine withdrawn Class 37s. This was one of the first of the Vulcan Foundry builds, emerging as D6718 in the summer of 1961, and becoming No. 37018 under TOPS. It was renumbered to 37517 in 1987, and is surely the class member to carry the longest name, *St Aidan's CE Memorial School Hartlepool Railsafe Trophy Winners 1995* – although perhaps for the shortest time, as the name was removed in 1996. (J. M. Walker)

No. 37059 at Attenborough

With what looks like a semi-fluorescent nose, DRS-liveried No. 37059 passes Attenborough on 5 August 2015 hauling a DVT unit from Norwich Crown Point to Loughborough.

No. 37423 at Carlisle

Revenue-earning passenger duty for No. 37423 *Spirit of the Lakes*, seen here at Carlisle in January 2016 at the rear of a Lancaster service, which has a Driving Van Trailer at the other end. No. 37423 was originally D6996 and later No. 37296. Conversion to Class 37/4 at Crewe took place in 1986. It was once named *Sir Murray Morrison 1873–1948 Pioneer of British Aluminium Industry*.

No. 37290 at Sheffield

No. 37290 arrives at Sheffield with a Skegness–Manchester service on 10 September 1983. Released to traffic as D6990, it was rebuilt as No. 37411 in 1985. It was named *The Institution of Railway Engineers* in 1987 and then *Caerphilly Castle/Castell Caerffili* in 2005. Withdrawn in 2013, it was cut up at Booth's of Rotherham. One of the cabs now graces the car park of the Alexandra Hotel in Derby. (J. M. Walker)

Nos 37899 and 37896 at Brookhouse, South Yorkshire

Another view of No. 37899 *Sir Gorllewin Morgannwg/County of West Glamorgan* and No. 37896 on the Bolsover Balladeer special at Brookhouse on the South Yorkshire Joint Line, 1 September 1991.

No. 37010 at Doncaster

A King's Cross–Newcastle service pulls into Doncaster on 17 July 1979, with No. 37010 leading failed No. 47405. Built at Vulcan Foundry as D6710, this was the locomotive that pulled off a more notable rescue ten years before this picture, when it banked the stranded No. 4472 *Flying Scotsman* on the notorious incline out of Barnsley on the Penistone branch.

No. 37079 at Sheffield

No. 37079 stands at Sheffield station on 4 August 1984 with the empty stock of a summer Saturday service. This was an RSH build, released to traffic as D6779 in late 1962. It carried the number 37357 briefly in the late 1980s, but reverted to No. 37079 in 1990. (J. M. Walker)

No. 37009 at Thornaby

No. 37009 was stabled at Thornaby depot on Saturday 8 November 1980. Built at Vulcan Foundry, it was released new to Stratford in February 1961. Unofficially named *Typhoon* at Tinsley in 1989, and renumbered to 37340 in 1994, it survives in preservation.

Nos 37031 and 37078 at Mitchell's Main

A Dodworth–Wath working approaches Mitchell's Main near Wombwell in the summer of 1983, with Nos 37031 and 37078 in charge. No. 37031 was a relatively early withdrawal, being taken out of service in 1994 and cut up in 1997. No. 37078 emerged from the RSH plant a year after its partner and was delivered new to Thornaby. It too was withdrawn in 1994. (J. M. Walker)

Nos 37007 and 37067 at Stairfoot

A Dodworth–Wath Yard MGR working approaches Stairfoot on the outskirts of Barnsley in July 1983, with Nos 37007 and 37067 in charge. No. 37007 was refurbished in 1986 and became No. 37506, after which it was named *British Steel Skinningrove*; a further change to No. 37604 occurred in 1995. No. 37067 was renumbered to 37703 in 1987 and later spent three years in Spain. (V. Hellam)

Nos 37024/030 at Clay Cross

Nos 37024 and 37030 storm through Clay Cross with a steel coil working on 9 June 1983. No. 37024 was built at Vulcan Foundry in August 1961 as D6724. It carried the number 37024 from 1974 to 1988 and then became No. 37714. No. 37030 was originally D6730. It became No. 37701 in 1986. (J. M. Walker)

No. 37294 at Inverness

In 'Dutch' Civil Engineer's livery, No. 37294 stands in one of the bays at Inverness station on 24 August 1993. (J. M. Walker)

No. 37259 at Doncaster

No. 37259 marshalls an engineer's train at Doncaster in January 1985. This locomotive was built at Vulcan Foundry in January 1965, and was first allocated to Darnall before moving to Wath later that year. It was renumbered to 37388 in 1988 but assumed its previous identity in 2002 when it was allocated to the DRS fleet at Carlisle.

No. 37245 at Shirebrook

No. 37245 was among several of the class stabled at Shirebrook on 30 May 1983. This was a Vulcan Foundry machine built in October 1964 as D6945. It suffered severe damage in a collision in 1987 but was repaired at Crewe and served for a further thirteen years before being scrapped at Wigan. (J. M. Walker)

Nos 37164 and 37161 at Thornaby

Thornaby TMD on 8 November 1980, with Nos 37164 and 37161 outside the shed. No. 37161 was renumbered to 37899 in 1987 and then went to Spain in 2001. It never returned to the UK, being cut up in Madrid in 2003. No. 37164 became No. 37675 in 1987. It carried the name *William Cookworthy* between 1987 and 1994 (previously carried by No. 37207).

Nos 37799 and 37220 at Forteviot

Nos 37799 and 37220 head past Forteviot, south of Perth, with a Speedlink working from Aberdeen to Mossend on 30 June 1999. No. 37220 later carried the name *Westerleigh* and survived in service until 2005. No. 37799 was built as D6761 and became No. 37061 in 1974. It was renumbered to 37799 in 1986 and was later named *Sir Dyfed/County of Dyfed*. (V. Hellam)

No. 37518 at Clay Cross

No. 37518 heads south through Clay Cross with a mixed freight on 26 August 1988. Built by RSH in 1962, and released to traffic as D6776, this locomotive was first allocated to Thornaby. It was renumbered to 37076 in 1974 and then as 37518 in 1987.

No. 37680 at Buxton

Sporting Railfreight Construction sector livery, No. 37680 stands at Buxton stabling point on 1 September 1992, in the company of No. 37416. The former No. 37224, built at Vulcan Foundry as D6924 in January 1964, was rebuilt as 37680 at Crewe in 1987. (J. M. Walker)

Nos 37261 and 37422 at Barrow Hill

Nos 37261 and 37422 stand in the yard at Barrow Hill on 8 February 2014. No. 37261 was built at Vulcan Foundry in January 1965 and was delivered new to Darnall. Later named *Caithness*, it spent time on hire in France from 1999 to 2000. No. 37422 was originally D6966, a Vulcan Foundry machine built in February 1965. Later No. 37266, it became No. 37422 in 1986 and was allocated to Carlisle Kingmoor in 2011.

No. 37123 at Sheffield

No. 37123 stands at Sheffield with a summer Saturday service on 7 July 1984, this time bringing holidaymakers home from Scarborough to Nottingham. Later No. 37679, this locomotive was bought for preservation in 2007. (J. M. Walker)

No. 37126 at Ravensthorpe

How summer Saturdays used to be – the former D6826, here seen in its familiar rail blue livery as No. 37126, passes Ravensthorpe with the Sheffield–Blackpool service on 27 August 1983. Later renumbered to 37676, it was named *Loch Rannoch* in 2008 and was still in service in 2015, as part of the WCR fleet. (V. Hellam)

Nos 37886 and 37684 at Crewe TMD

No. 37886 stands at Crewe TMD alongside classmate No. 37684 in August 2001. No. 37886 was originally D6880, built at the RSH foundry and delivered new to Landore in October 1963. As No. 37180 it carried the name *Sir Dyfed – County of Dyfed* from 1981 to 1987. Conversion to No. 37886 came in 1988, and its name was reinstated in 2001. No. 37684 was delivered new from Vulcan Foundry in the spring of 1963. First numbered D6834, it became No. 37134 in 1974 and then No. 37684 in 1987.

No. 37610 at Derby

Shortly after being named *The Malcolm Group*, No. 37610 runs light through Derby in September 2002. Built by RSH and delivered new as D6881 in October 1963, this locomotive did not become No. 37610 until 1995, before which it carried the identities No. 37181 (from 1974) and No. 37687 (from 1987). It was named *T. S. (Ted) Cassady 14.5.61 – 6.4.08* in 2008.

Nos 37504 and 37202 at Brancliffe East Junction

Nos 37504 and 37202 are seen at Brancliffe East Junction on 5 September 1993. No. 37504 was built in May 1962 as D6739, later becoming No. 37039. In 1986 it became No. 37504, and was named *British Steel Corby*, a name it carried until 1991 when it was named *Fort William/An Gearasdan*. In 1996 it was renumbered to 37603. No. 37202 later became No. 37331.

No. 37359 at Peak Forest

No. 37359 runs light engine past the signal box at Peak Forest sidings on 14 June 1993. This was a Vulcan Foundry machine built in March 1963 and delivered new to Darnall as D6818. It became No. 37118 under the TOPS scheme in 1974, then No. 37359 in 1988. It was cut up at Carnforth in 2005.

No. 37246 at Wath shed

No. 37246 rests outside the shed at Wath with No. 45022 on 23 May 1982. Built at Vulcan Foundry, it was delivered new to Cardiff Canton as D6946 in 1964. It was rebuilt at Crewe in 1986, emerging from the works as No. 37698. It later sported Railfreight coal sector livery, during which time it carried the name *Coedbach*.

No. 37172 at Wakefield Kirkgate

No. 37172 runs light engine through Wakefield Kirkgate on 26 June 1979. Emerging from Vulcan Foundry as D6872 in September 1963, it became No. 37172 in 1974 and then No. 37686 in 1987. After a stint on hire in France at the end of the 1990s, it was stored as unserviceable, finally being cut up in 2006.

Nos 37188 and 37152 at Rowsley South

Nos 37152 and 37188 stand at Rowsley on the Peak Railway in 2015. No. 37152 was built at Vulcan Foundry as D6852 in July 1963. It was renumbered to 37152 in 1974 and then to 37310 in 1986, when it was named *British Steel Ravenscraig*. It reverted to No. 37152 in 1989. No. 37188 was an RSH machine, built as D6888 in January 1964. Named *Jimmy Shand* in 1985, it was sold for preservation in 2003.

No. 37219 at Basford Hall Yard, Crewe

No. 37219 stands next to No. 58050 in the yard at Basford Hall, Crewe, on 27 August 1995. No. 37219 was built at Vulcan Foundry in January 1964 as D6919. Withdrawn in 2005, it moved to the Gloucestershire Warwickshire Railway in 2007 and was later named *Shirley Ann Smith*.

Nos 37138, 37051 and 37053 at Carlisle

A trio of Railfreight-liveried 37s stands at Carlisle on 13 August 1992. No. 37138 entered traffic in the spring of 1963 and after forty years' service was scrapped at Toton in 2004. No. 37051 emerged from Vulcan Foundry in August 1962. From 1996 it carried the name *Merehead* and was cut up in 2008. No. 37053 became No. 37344 in 1994 and after a period of storage was cut up in 2006. (J. M. Walker)

No. 37401 at Crianlarich

No. 37401 stands at Crianlarich with a service for Fort William on 26 August 1989. The original D6968, it became No. 37268 in 1974 and then No. 37401 in 1985. (V. Hellam)

No. 37608 at Attenborough

With sister No. 37606 on the rear, DRS-liveried No. 37608 heads through Attenborough towards Derby with the Network Rail test train on 20 January 2016. Built in July 1961, No. 37608 emerged from the factory as D6722, later becoming No. 37022 under TOPS and then No. 37512 in 1987, in which guise it carried the name *Thornaby Demon*.

No. 37094 at Penistone

No. 37094 stands in the permanent way yard at Penistone on 24 October 1980. The split headcode boxes of this Vulcan Foundry built machine later disappeared when it was refurbished and numbered 37716 in 1988. It was allocated to the DRS fleet at Kingmoor in 2013. (V. Hellam)

No. 37058 at Attenborough

No. 37058, carrying two-tone grey livery, is seen here passing Attenborough with a short train of cement tanks on 23 May 1989. It was dispatched to France in 1999, and was withdrawn ten years later, being cut up at C. F. Booth in Rotherham in 2009.

No. 37024 at Treeton South

No. 37024 passes Treeton South with a bulk oil working on 2 July 1982. Built at Vulcan Foundry in August 1961 as D6724, it was later rebuilt at Crewe as a heavyweight 37/7, emerging from the works in 1988 as No. 37714. It carried the name *Thornaby TMD* between 1992 and 1993 and was later hired to Spain. On its return, No. 37714 became part of the DRS fleet.

No. 37089 at Horbury

No. 37089 heads through Horbury Cutting with the Healey Mills breakdown train in June 1982. An RSH machine, it was delivered new to Gateshead as D6789 in 1963. It carried the number 37089 from 1974 to 1988, when it was converted to No. 37708. It was despatched to France from 1999 to 2000, but on its return only survived a further seven years.

No. 37292 at Dringhouses, York

No. 37292 approaches York with the Doncaster Works test train in September 1981. This locomotive was built at Vulcan Foundry in July 1965 and emerged as D6992. After a heavy general overhaul in 1986 it was renumbered to 37425, becoming part of the Regional Railways pool, and was named *Sir Robert MacAlpine/ Concrete Bob* at Fort William that year.

No. 37688 at Moorthorpe

Moorthorpe station on 6 May 1993, and No. 37688 *Great Rocks* stands with a rake of open wagons during maintenance work. A Vulcan Foundry build, it was released to traffic as D6905 in November 1963. It became No. 37205 under TOPS and was renumbered to 37688 in 1987. Named *Kingmoor TMD* in 2007, it was still in traffic in 2016 as part of the DRS fleet. (J. M. Walker)

Nos 37075 and 37101 at Great Rocks Junction

On 6 August 1985, Nos 37075 and 37101 are held on the approach to Great Rocks Junction while working light engine to Buxton. No. 37075 was one of the RSH batch, delivered new to Thornaby as D6775 in September 1962. It was sold into preservation in 1999. (J. M. Walker)

No. 37207 at Peak Forest sidings

Cardiff Canton based No. 37207 is seen here at Peak Forest in June 1988. Built at Vulcan Foundry in 1963, its first home depot was Landore. It was named *William Cookworthy* in 1982 but the nameplates had been removed by 1987. Withdrawn in 1999, No. 37207 went into preservation at the Plym Valley Railway before moving to Barrow Hill.

No. 37072 at Bamford

No. 37072 powers through Bamford on the Hope Valley with 1M54, the summer Saturday service from Skegness to Manchester, in August 1983. Built as D6772 by RSH, this locomotive had a single central headcode panel fitted at the No. 1 end following damage sustained in a collision with No. 31102 in 1986. It later carried the unofficial name *Venom* while allocated to Tinsley.

No. 37101 at Woodburn Junction, Sheffield

No. 37101 is seen here on a light engine move at Woodburn Junction in July 1983. It was built as D6801 and delivered new from Vulcan Foundry to Darnall depot in December 1962. It became No. 37345 in 1994 but was condemned in 1998 and cut up at Immingham in 2003.

No. 37063 at Sheffield

No. 37063 basks in the sunshine at Sheffield on 25 August 1984. It is standing at the head of a Manchester Piccadilly service, something normally the preserve of the Class 31/4s. After a lengthy period in storage, No. 37063 was finally cut up at Kingsbury in 2001. (J. M. Walker)

No. 37084 at Chinley

Storming upgrade on the approach to Chinley, No. 37084 heads a rake of classic ICI aggregate hoppers en route to the Peak Forest on 31 August 1984. This was one of the RSH batch, built in December 1962 as D6784 and delivered new to Gateshead. It became No. 37718 in 1989. (J. M. Walker)

Nos 37681 and 37686 at Great Rocks Junction

Nos 37681 and 37686 power away from Great Rocks Junction towards Peak Forest with a loaded aggregates working on 17 June 1988. Sisters Nos 37678 and 37684 head for Buxton in the distance. All four locomotives were based at Tinsley at the time.

No. 37283 at Goose Hill Junction

No. 37283 sweeps through Normanton and towards Goose Hill Junction with a summer Saturday passenger service on 6 August 1983. No. 37283 later became No. 37895 after a rebuild at Crewe and, after a spell of cross-Channel duty, it was scrapped in 2011. (V. Hellam)

No. 37052 at Barnsley

No. 37052 takes a sand train for Stairfoot through Barnsley station on 31 October 1983. Another of the 'split box' 37s later converted to a 37/7, No. 37052 was delivered new to Darnall shed as D6752 in 1962. It became No. 37713 in 1988 and was later named *British Steel Workington*. (V. Hellam)

No. 37062 at Church Fenton

Classic station architecture frames No. 37062 trundling south at Church Fenton with a ballast train on 17 April 1984. It later carried the name *British Steel Corby*. This particular locomotive met a premature end after a collision in 1989 and was scrapped by Vic Berry at Leicester in 1990. (J. M. Walker)

Nos 37678 and 37684 at Peak Forest sidings

Nos 37678 and 37684 head away from Peak Forest sidings on 17 June 1988. No. 37678 was originally D6956 (later No. 37256). It was withdrawn in 2007 and cut up at Kingsbury. No. 37684 was originally D6834 (later 37134). While also withdrawn in 2007, it was a further three years before it was cut up at C. F. Booth of Rotherham.

No. 37044 at Doncaster Works

No. 37044 is seen here undergoing a static dynamometer test at Doncaster Works during the 1984 Open Day. This locomotive had a long association with 'the Plant', making numerous visits for maintenance over the years, although its conversion to a 37/7 in 1988 was carried out at Crewe.

No. 37025 at Kyle of Lochalsh

No. 37025 stands opposite the Viking Bar at Kyle of Lochalsh station, having arrived with an early morning service from Inverness that carried both passengers and mail, on a cool and damp 25 June 1985.

No. 37219 at Warrington

No. 37219, in Mainline blue livery, is seen at Arpley stabling point on 21 April 2000. Built at Vulcan Foundry in 1964 as D6919, its original career came to an end when it was sold for preservation in 2007, but it was acquired by Colas Railfreight in 2014 and has subsequently returned once more to the national network. (V. Hellam)

No. 37684 at Crewe

No. 37684 *Peak National Park* accelerates through Crewe station en route to the Stockport lines in September 2001. Built at Vulcan Foundry in April 1963 as D6834, it was delivered new to Cardiff Canton depot. It became No. 37134 under the 1974 TOPS scheme and then No. 37684 in 1987.

No. 37171 at Wakefield Kirkgate

No. 37171 stands at Kirkgate station on 26 June 1979. This Vulcan Foundry built machine was delivered to traffic as D6871 and, after the obligatory period in corporate rail blue, was converted to No. 37690 in 1987. It was further modified for European Passenger Service duties in 1995, taking on the identity No. 37611.

No. 37088 at Sheffield

No. 37088 stands on one of Sheffield's centre roads in the spring of 1982. Built at RSH in January 1963 as D6788, it was first allocated to Gateshead. It was renumbered to No. 37088 in 1974 and then No. 37323 in 1986, before reverting to No. 37088 in 1989.

Nos 37091 and 37020 at Chesterfield

Nos 37091 and 37020 take a train of steel coil south at Chesterfield on 24 August 1983. Built by RSH in 1963, No. 37091 was later renumbered to 37358 and named *P&O Containers*. (J. M. Walker)

Nos 37012 and 37101 at Doncaster Works

Among three Class 37s in view at Doncaster in May 1980 are Nos 37012 and 37101. Built at Vulcan Foundry in 1961 and 1962 respectively, both were withdrawn and scrapped in 2003. No. 37012 retained its first TOPS identity to the end, whereas No. 37101 was renumbered to 37345 in 1994.

Nos 37710, 37694 and 37344 at Healey Mills

On 30 April 1995, three Class 37s stand outside the shed at Healey Mills. No. 37710 was previously No. 37044, built at Vulcan Foundry in June 1962; No. 37694 was No. 37192, built by RSH in 1964 and later named *The Lass O' Ballochmyle*; No. 37344 was once No. 37053, built at Vulcan Foundry in September 1962. All three were scrapped between 2006 and 2008. (V. Hellam)

No. 37096 at Doncaster Works

In the company of a newly built Class 58, No. 37096 is seen in sparkling condition following a repaint at Doncaster on 25 August 1983. This was on the occasion of its final classified repair at the works. (J. M. Walker)

No. 37106 at Lincoln Central

No. 37106 enjoys some early summer sunshine while stabled at Lincoln on 27 May 1987. Emerging from Vulcan Foundry in January 1963, D6806 was delivered new to Darnall. It became a relatively early candidate for withdrawal and was sent to Wigan as part of the EWS 'condemned pool' in 1999.

No. 37226 at Sheffield

Sheffield station on 20 August 1983, and Tinsley stalwart No. 37226, by this stage equipped with miniature snowploughs, stands with a summer Saturday train, having arrived from the east coast. (J. M. Walker)

No. 37170 at Crianlarich

An inspection saloon forms a lightweight load for 'Dutch'-liveried No. 37170 at Crianlarich station on 17 August 1994. No. 37170 was withdrawn in 2005 but was reinstated to traffic as part of the Network Rail civil engineer's fleet, fully refurbished and numbered No. 97302. (V. Hellam)

No. 37115 at Doncaster

No. 37115, still sporting 'domino' headcode inserts, and with nose-end doors yet to be plated over, stands at Doncaster station in 1986. Built at Vulcan Foundry and delivered new to Darnall in 1963 as D6815, it became No. 37514 in 1987, and then No. 37609 in 1995 as part of the EPS fleet.

Nos 37226 and 37218 at Dodworth

On a late summer's evening at Dodworth in 1982, Tinsley's Nos 37226 and 37218 pull away from the colliery with a loaded MGR service for Wath. No. 37226 was cut up at Booth's of Rotherham in 2008, but No. 37218 was still in traffic in 2016, more than fifty years after it emerged from Vulcan Foundry in the first weeks of 1964.

No. 37207 at Peak Forest sidings

Cardiff Canton based No. 37207 is seen here engaged in a spot of shunting at Peak Forest in preparation for working a loaded aggregates train. Built at Vulcan Foundry and released to traffic in November 1963, its first home depot was Landore. Withdrawn in 1999, No. 37207 initially went into preservation at the Plym Valley Railway.

No. 37101 at Guide Bridge

Guide Bridge station is seen here on a hazy 2 September 1983, with No. 37101 at the head of a train of scrap metal comprising a rake of 16-ton mineral wagons. This locomotive became No. 37345 in 1994, but was condemned in 1998 and was cut up Immingham in 2003. (V. Hellam)

No. 37121 at Sheffield

No. 37121 heads a train of mineral wagons through Sheffield in July 1982. Built by RSH and released to traffic as D6821 in the spring of 1963, it was refurbished in 1987, becoming No. 37677. It was surplus to operating requirements by 2004 and went into storage before being withdrawn in 2008.

No. 37097 at Sheffield

No. 37097 trundles light engine through Sheffield in July 1982. Built at Vulcan Foundry, this locomotive emerged in December 1962 as D6797 and was allocated first to Darnall. Here it is with nose-end doors still *in situ* and front valance extending around the buffers.

No. 37121 at Wath Yard

Tinsley's No. 37121 pauses at the eastern end of Wath Yard on 25 June 1982. This was one of the RSH batch, entering traffic in April 1963 as D6821. It carried the number 37121 for a further five years after the date of this picture, being renumbered to 37677 in 1987.

No. 37058 at Newton Harcourt, Leicestershire

In two-tone grey livery, No. 37058 heads an excursion from St Pancras to Leicester on 21 May 1989. Built at Vulcan Foundry in October 1962, D6758 was delivered new to Thornaby. It spent time in France at the turn of the century and was withdrawn and cut up at Rotherham in 2009.

No. 37228 at Cudworth

This is the former Midland main line at Cudworth in November 1982 with No. 37228 hauling withdrawn 'Peaks' Nos 46006 and 46007 to Swindon for scrapping. Built at Vulcan Foundry as D6928 in February 1964, this locomotive later carried the number 37696. It was cut up at Booth's in Rotherham in late 2014.

No. 37248 at Tinsley depot

No. 37248 is seen at Tinsley on 8 June 1993. Delivered new to Cardiff Canton as D6948 in 1964, No. 37248 was named *Midland Railway Centre* in 1995 and went into preservation ten years later. It was beautifully restored into green livery at the Gloucestershire & Warwickshire Railway in 2015, its days in shabby two-tone grey long gone.

No. 37211 at Tinsley

Lonely as a cloud... No. 37211, in Railfreight Construction sub-sector livery and with small snowploughs, arrives at what remains of Tinsley yard in April 1993. Up in the shed yard above, No. 37032 *Mirage* can be seen. (J. M. Walker)

Nos 37010 and 37185 at Peak Forest

Nos 37010 and 37185 are seen here shunting at Peak Forest in September 1983. No. 37185, an RSH machine built in December 1963, carried the unofficial name *Buccaneer* from 1989 to 1991 and was then named *Lea & Perrins* in 1993. (V. Hellam)

No. 37058 at Attenborough

No. 37058 looks to have had a recent front-end repaint in this image from 14 June 1989. It is seen passing Attenborough with a mixed consist of scrap metal and cement, both loads originating in nearby Beeston.

No. 37601 at Attenborough

The 09.35 Derby–York Network Rail service approaches Attenborough station on the morning of Monday 28 July 2014. Vehicle 9701 is leading, with No. 37601 (the former No. 37005/37501) propelling.

Nos 37607 and 37218 at Closeburn

A Pathfinders Tours' charter heads past Closeburn on the G&SW route with Nos 37607 and 37218 on 6 April 2015. No. 37607 was released to traffic as D6803, later becoming No. 37103 and then No. 37511. It was renumbered to 37607 in 1995 as part of the EPS fleet. No. 37218 has carried the same number since 1974, when its TOPS identity superseded the original D6918. (V. Hellam)

No. 37083 at Goose Hill Junction

Four coke hoppers and a brake van make up a lightweight load for No. 37083, seen heading south at Goose Hill Junction on a misty 11 July 1983, possibly destined for Royston. Delivered new as D6783 in December 1962, this RSH built machine was later allocated to the Civil Engineer's fleet. (V. Hellam)

No. 37097 at Healey Mills

No. 37097 departs a rather murky Healey Mills Yard with an eastbound freight in the winter of 1987. This was a Vulcan Foundry machine, built in December 1962 and delivered new to Darnall. It was sold to the Caledonian Railway in 2003 and named *Old Fettercairn* at Brechin in 2007.

No. 37084 at Chinley

A swathe of willow herb frames No. 37084 as it works an empty aggregates service at Chinley on 31 August 1984. Originally the RSH built D6784, it later became No. 37718 and then L021 for transfer to Spain in 2001, returning to the UK in 2007. (V. Hellam)

No. 37002 at Huddersfield

No. 37002 is seen on a ballast working at Huddersfield on 6 October 1981. This was one of Vulcan Foundry's very early builds, emerging from the works in December 1960. It became No. 37351 in 1989 and served for a further eighteen years before withdrawal in 2007.

No. 37697 at Aylesbury

No. 37697 is seen here at Aylesbury while working passenger shuttles to and from Princes Risborough on 20 June 1987. Built at Vulcan Foundry and released to traffic as D6943, this locomotive was renumbered to 37243 under TOPS and became No. 37697 after a heavy general overhaul at Crewe in 1986. It was scrapped in 2006. (V. Hellam)

Nos 37010 and 37242 at Penistone

Nos 37010 and 37242 storm through Penistone on 16 July 1981 with a container service bound for Swansea. Both were built at Vulcan Foundry, No. 37010 (D6710) in February 1961 and No. 37242 (D6942) in September 1964. No. 37010 worked in France between 1999 and 2000 and was withdrawn and cut up in 2007. No. 37242 was withdrawn in 1999 and, after a period of storage, was cut up in 2006.

No. 37025 at Inverness

There was still plenty of period detail to be found at Inverness in June 1985, when this image of No. 37025 was captured. The loco is seen threading its way between the semaphores prior to working a Kyle of Lochalsh turn.

No. 37082 at Horbury

16 September 1984, and No. 37082 stands at the head of an engineer's train just outside Healey Mills yard. This machine was one of the RSH batch and was released to traffic as D6782 in November 1962. It became No. 37082 in 1974, and then No. 37502 in 1986. It was named *British Steel Teesside* in 1987, and was then converted to No. 37602 in 1995, joining the European Passenger Service fleet. (J. M. Walker)

No. 37713 at Doncaster Works

No. 37713 stands in the paint shop yard at Doncaster on 10 July 1994. The de-cluttered front end is illustrated to good effect here. Gone are the twin headcode boxes and in their place are recessed headlamps and central high-intensity light. This was a Vulcan Foundry locomotive, delivered new as D6752 in September 1962. It became No. 37713 in 1988 and carried the name *British Steel Workington* from 1992 to 1994.

No. 37905 at Doncaster works

The Class 37/9s were fitted with either Ruston or Mirrlees engines in place of the original English Electric power plant. This is the original D6836, built in April 1963, and later becoming No. 37136 under the TOPS scheme. Conversion to No. 37905 took place at Crewe in 1986, and it was named *Vulcan Enterprise* in 1987. (V. Hellam)

Appendix

The Class 37s – technical details (as built)

Constructor: English Electric and Robert Stephenson & Hawthorns Ltd
Engine type: EE 12CSVT
Wheel layout: Co-Co
Weight: 102 to 108 tonnes
Length: 61 ft 6 in
Horsepower: 1750
Power at rail (hp): 1250
Tractive effort: 55,500 lb
Brake force: 50 tonnes
Maximum speed: 90 mph (later reduced to 80 mph)
No. of traction motors: 6
Brake type: vacuum (dual brakes fitted from 1970s onwards)
Fuel capacity: 1690 gal
Route availability: 5

The sub-class variants

Class 37/3 – 37330 to 37384

Converted from the original fleet in 1988
No train heating
Tractive effort increased to 56,180 lb
Weight: 106 tonnes

Class 37/4 – 37401 to 37431

Converted from the original fleet in 1985/86
Electric train heating fitted
Steam heating removed
Tractive effort increased to 57,440 lb
Weight: 107 tonnes

Class 37/5 – 37501 to 37521 and 37667 to 37699

Converted from the original fleet in 1986/88
No train heating
Tractive effort increased to 55,590 lb
Weight: 107 tonnes

Class 37/6 – 37601 to 37612

Converted from the original fleet in 1994/96
Heating type through wired; air brake only
Coupling type: Blue Star/special for European Passenger Services fleet
Weight: 106 tonnes
Maximum speed: 90 mph

Class 37/7 – 37701 to 37719; 37796 to 37803 and 37883 to 37899

Converted from the original fleet in 1986/88
No train heating
Modified traction alternators
Additional ballast
Tractive effort increased to 61,910 lb
Route availability 7
Weight: 120 tonnes

Class 37/9 – 37901 to 37906

Converted from the original fleet in 1986/87
Engines: Mirrlees MB275T (37901-904); Ruston RX270T (37905-06)
No train heating
Modified traction alternators
Additional ballast
Tractive effort increased to 62,680 lb
Route availability 7
Weight: 120 tonnes